The Story of Our Holidays

MARDI GRAS

Joanna Ponto

Enslow Publishing
101 W. 23rd Street
Suite 240
New York, NY 10011
USA
enslow.com

Published in 2016 by Enslow Publishing, LLC.
101 W. 23rd Street, Suite 240, New York, NY 10011

Library of Congress Cataloging-in-Publication Data

Ponto, Joanna.
  Mardi Gras / Joanna Ponto.
      pages cm — (The story of our holidays)
  Includes bibliographical references and index.
  ISBN 978-0-7660-7460-6 (library binding)
  ISBN 978-0-7660-7472-9 (pbk.)
  ISBN 978-0-7660-7466-8 (6-pack)
  1. Carnival—Louisiana—New Orleans—Juvenile literature. 2. New Orleans (La.)—Social life and customs—Juvenile literature. 3. New Orleans (La.)—Social life and customs. I. Title.
  GT4211.N4P66 2015
  394.2509763'35—dc23
                            2015030383

Printed in the United States of America

To Our Readers: We have done our best to make sure all website addresses in this book were active and appropriate when we went to press. However, the author and the publisher have no control over and assume no liability for the material available on those websites or on any websites they may link to. Any comments or suggestions can be sent by e-mail to customerservice@enslow.com.

Portions of this book originally appeared in the book *Mardi Gras: Parades, Costumes, and Parties.*

Photos Credits: Cover, p. 1 Mike Flippo/Shutterstock.com; p. 4 © AP Images; p. 6 David Grunfeld/ The Times-Picayune/Landov; p. 10 © Look and Learn/Bridgeman Images; p. 14 Chris Graythen/Getty Images/Thinkstock; p. 16 Cheryl Gerber/Getty Images/Thinkstock; p. 19 Ben Gabbe/Getty Images Entertainment/Getty Images; p. 21 Skip Bolen/Getty Images Entertainment/Getty Images; p. 23 Richard Ellis/Getty Images News/Getty Images; p. 24 bonchan/Shutterstock.com; p. 26 CaseyMartin/ Shutterstock.com; pp. 29 Karen Huang; p. 30 Erika J Mitchell/Shutterstock.com.

Contents

This masker wears a costume that looks like a snake during a Mardi Gras parade in New Orleans.

Chapter 1

A Night for Fun!

The sun sets on a street filled with dancers. Music fills the air in New Orleans, Louisiana. People are ready to party.

Meet the Maskers

A parade comes down the street. The people in the parade are called maskers. They are all wearing masks and brightly colored costumes decorated with sparkling beads or feathers. Several maskers wear huge gold, green, or purple hats called headdresses.

The maskers ride on large colorful floats that look like small stages on wheels. Tractors slowly pull them down the street.

On one float, people are riding a large golden dragon. On another, a man and a woman are dressed like a king and a

The floats for Mardi Gras are often eye-catching with special effects and bright colors.

queen. They have helpers with them. There is also a large white horse made of plaster that is covered with flowers. Everything on the float sparkles. The night sky seems to light up.

People watching the parade wear costumes, too. Everyone is happy and laughing. This is a night for fun. The crowd calls out to the maskers, "Throw me something, Mister."

The maskers toss small gifts from their floats to the crowd. Hard candies and small plastic Frisbees fly through the air. People are wearing strings of plastic beads that have been tossed to them. They quickly scoop up colorful coins from the street. Some people bring shopping bags to carry all the treats being thrown to them.

These last few days have been great. There were parties, wonderful meals, and music. But the parade was the best part. No one will ever forget this magical celebration. It was Mardi Gras (MAR dee GRAH).

An Extra-Special Holiday

Mardi Gras is a special holiday. There is no other quite like it. Holidays are celebrated in many different ways. There are parades every July 4. Thanksgiving Day dinners are fun. New Year's Eve is known for its parties. On Halloween people wear costumes.

But Mardi Gras is the only holiday when all these things are done. It is a time for make-believe and having fun. It is also a time for good food and good friends. It is like no other time of the year.

In the United States, Mardi Gras is celebrated in some areas of the South. Many of these places are near the Gulf of Mexico. A few of the larger Mardi Gras celebrations are in New Orleans, Louisiana; Mobile, Alabama; and Galveston, Texas. But the holiday is celebrated in other places, too.

Chapter 2

Historic Holiday

The first Mardi Gras celebration was held in Europe hundreds of years ago. Celebrating Mardi Gras was a way to welcome spring. People saw spring as a new beginning. They danced, sang, and feasted. Everyone hoped for good crops, healthy farm animals, happiness, and wealth.

Time for a Party

Mardi Gras is always held before Lent. Lent is an important time for Christians. It is not a celebration. It is a time for prayer. People ask for forgiveness for their sins.

Lent lasts for six weeks. Christians used to give up meat, cheese, and butter during Lent. People often fasted, which means not eating at all.

Mardi Gras is French for Fat Tuesday. The last day of celebration during the Mardi Gras season occurs on the last Tuesday before Lent. It does not fall on the same day each year. The holiday can be any time from February 3 to March 9. But it is always forty-seven days before Easter.

In some places, Mardi Gras is called Carnival. The word carnival comes from the Latin words *carne vale*, meaning farewell to meat. It is a time to eat whatever you can before fasting for the Lenten season.

Let's Get This Party Started: Twelfth Night

There is a whole Carnival season that begins every year on January 6. That date is also known as Twelfth Night because it is twelve days after Christmas. Some Christians believe that the Three Wise Men visited the baby Jesus at that time.

Twelfth Night is the start of the Mardi Gras or Carnival season. That is when the parties and fun begin. The celebrating is in full swing by Fat Tuesday. Then, at the stroke of midnight, the celebration is over and Lent starts.

It is possible that the name Mardi Gras comes from the French tradition of parading a fat ox through town.

In some parts of the United States, Mardi Gras has been celebrated for more than two hundred years. In 1699, French explorers had been traveling down the Mississippi River. They stopped about sixty miles from what is now New Orleans, Louisiana.

The date was March 3. The men missed their homes and families. They knew that Mardi Gras was being celebrated in France. So they named the spot where they stopped *Pointe du Mardi Gras* (Mardi Gras Point).

When French people settled in the area, Mardi Gras celebrations began. One settlement started in Mobile, Alabama. In 1703, the new settlers held the country's first Mardi Gras celebration.

Over time, the celebration grew. There were balls and dances. People came in costumes and masks. They danced until late at night. Mobile has been called the City That Started It All.

Several years later, the French began a settlement in Louisiana. It was known as *Nouvelle Orleans* (New Orleans). Mardi Gras became popular there, too. In time, New Orleans would become famous for its Mardi Gras celebrations.

Today these celebrations have grown and changed. Thousands of people now enjoy Mardi Gras. Some people live in areas where there are Mardi Gras festivals. Other people are visitors. No one wants to miss the fun.

France's Carnival

A large Carnival celebration is held every year in Nice, which is in the French Riviera. Everyone attends parties, parades, and masquerade balls.

Chapter 3

Parades Day and Night

Some areas hold a city-wide Mardi Gras party. Sometimes these parties take place in the streets before the Mardi Gras parades begin.

Mardi Gras parades are famous. Some areas have parades throughout Mardi Gras season, both day and night.

Each parade celebrates something different. It may be about a famous person or an important event. Sometimes the parade is about a local legend.

Some Mardi Gras parades are big. They may have more than three thousand people and have floats as tall as a building!

The people riding the floats wear fantastic costumes and masks. Often people play musical instruments on the floats, while a marching band follows behind. There may also be magicians, dancers, clowns, and motorcycle riders, too.

In the Club: Krewes

Special Mardi Gras clubs put on the parades. In most places, these clubs are known as krewes. But in Mobile, Alabama, the groups are called Mystic Societies.

The different krewes have interesting names. Many are named after ancient gods. One is called Aphrodite, the Greek the goddess of love. Another krewe is called Thor, the Norse god of war and thunder.

Krewes have a long history. They started in 1857, when a few young men from New Orleans formed the first one. They called it the Mistick Krewe of Comus. Comus was a Greek god of festivals and nightlife.

The men from the first krewe built two large floats that were pulled by horses. They dressed in costumes and masks. After dark, the Mistick Krewe of Comus paraded through the streets. Their servants carried lit torches and walked next to the floats. People came out to see the parade. They clapped, cheered, and were happy for the festivities.

The Mardi Gras king's and queen's costumes are usually the most spectacular.

In time, more krewes formed to celebrate Mardi Gras in many ways. Most krewes put on parades. Through the years, the parades became a custom. Now when people think of Mardi Gras, they often think of the wonderful parades.

Today there are many krewes in different cities. Each krewe has a captain, the krewe's leader. Others in the krewe have special roles, too. A krewe king and queen are picked each year to watch over the parade.

Usually the king and queen are members of the krewe. But some krewes offer this honor to celebrities.

The Thrill of Throws

Mardi Gras parades are about more than the fancy floats and colorful costumes. The way the maskers treat the parade watchers is important, too. In other parades, float riders just wave and smile. But in Mardi Gras parades, they also toss small items to the crowd.

These items are known as throws. Throws include strings of colorful plastic beads, cups, small Frisbees, whistles, and candies.

Small colorful coins are always popular. The krewe's crest may be stamped on one side of the coin. The parade's theme is on the other.

In Mobile, Alabama, the maskers throw MoonPies, small round cakes filled with marshmallow and covered in chocolate icing.

Many people bring home their throws as souvenirs.

Parade watchers love to bring home throws. Some people turn an umbrella upside down and hold it up in hopes that it will be filled with throws.

Parade goers sometimes bring special ladders that have a small bench attached to the top. Often parents put children on the bench. They hold the ladder's sides to steady it. The child can see the parade and is in a good place to catch throws.

All parades are fun, but Mardi Gras parades may be the best of all.

Chapter 4

Krewes and Their Secrets

Krewes are mysterious. Many times, krewe members are kept secret. Yet some people are in more than one of these Carnival clubs.

Put on Your Dancing Shoes

All krewes are extremely busy during the Mardi Gras season. Many have a fancy ball. Sometimes people wear costumes. Other times the women wear long gowns, and the men come in tuxedos. But everyone wears great masks to the ball.

The krewe's Mardi Gras king and queen are usually chosen at the ball. At some balls, the krewe also puts on a play. The play matches the parade's theme.

Some of the newer krewes no longer have Mardi Gras balls. Instead, they have dinners at nice hotels or restaurants. The balls and dinners are only for krewe members and their guests. But the krewes want everyone to join them for the parades.

At first, krewes were only for men. However, women wanted their own Carnival clubs. So, female Mardi Gras krewes began. Today there are krewes with both male and female members. There are krewes for children. There are even krewes for pets! Of course the pet owners join in, too.

A Few Cool Krewes

The Krewe of the Munchkins. This krewe from Galveston, Texas, is for children. The members are between four and fourteen years old. About five hundred munchkins are in the krewe's parade, and there are at least thirteen floats.

The Krewe of Barkus and Meoux. This krewe, also from Galveston, Texas, is for pets. An animal shelter runs it. Each year, there is a parade of animals dressed in costumes.

There are mostly dogs and cats in the parade. However, sometimes monkeys, small ponies, and guinea pigs take part. The owners parade with their pets. Some people even have costumes to match their pets.

The Mystics of Time. In this Mobile, Alabama, krewe, there are three fire-breathing dragons that lead the Mardi Gras parade. The first dragon is 150 feet long. The next two are smaller. Maskers ride the dragon floats and toss throws to the crowd. The dragons breathe real fire and smoke.

Costumes are an important part of Mardi Gras.

Phunny Phorty Phellows. This New Orleans krewe is made up of about fifty men and women. The Phunny Phorty Phellows have a special job. They celebrate the start of the Carnival season. Each year on January 6, krewe members put on their costumes, get on a streetcar decorated for Mardi Gras, and ride along a Mardi Gras parade route.

Rex. This is probably the best-known Carnival krewe in New Orleans. Mardi Gras parades had always been at night. But in 1872, Rex had the first daytime parade.

The Rex parade is on Fat Tuesday. It is the main event. The parade has fabulous floats and great music. It is the most photographed Mardi Gras parade.

Rex came up with the official Mardi Gras colors—gold, green, and purple. Gold stands for power. Green is for faith. Purple is for justice.

Britain's Carnival

Dressed in colorful costumes, dancers parade through the streets of London, England. Carnival takes place every year in England, and thousands of people come to watch the parades.

Rex also gave Mardi Gras its official song, "If I Ever Cease to Love." The song has silly words. "If I ever cease to love, May cows lay eggs and fish grow legs."

The Rex parade also has the boeuf gras, or fatted ox. Many years ago, the krewe had a live ox in its parade. Now one made out of papier-mâché, which is a light, strong kind of paper mixed with glue, is used. The ox represents the very last meat eaten before Lent.

The Zulu Krew often dress in traditional voodoo-inspired costumes, such as this zombie.

Zulu. The Zulu Aid and Pleasure Club is an African American krewe. It was named after an African tribe. People look forward to this krewe's parades. There are usually more than twenty bands and many throws. The most valued throws are Zulu's hand-painted coconuts.

Chapter 5

Mardi Gras in the Country

There are many ways to celebrate Mardi Gras. People in the country enjoy Mardi Gras runs. It is a community event.

Trinidad's Celebrations

For two days each year in Port-of-Spain, Trinidad, people celebrate Carnival. This celebration features the world's best steel bands and calypsos. People dance and sing all night long!

Mardi Gras Run

People in costumes meet at a starting point. Some are on horseback or trucks. Others bring musical instruments. These costumed riders stop at different homes along the way to sing and dance. In return, they ask for food. This is known as begging.

Mardi Gras runs bring the whole community together.

The food will be used to make gumbo. Gumbo is a spicy stew made with meat and seafood served over rice. See page 24 for a recipe.

Sometimes the beggars are given a bag of rice, a sack of onions, or smoked sausage. But a chicken is the best prize. Usually the homeowner lets loose a live chicken for the beggars to catch. Some say this is the best show of all. Everything is done in fun.

By late afternoon, the costumed riders return to town. A crowd welcomes them. Others make a large pot of gumbo. No one goes home hungry. Afterward a band plays and people dance.

Seafood Gumbo*

Ingredients:

3 tablespoons (15mL) butter or bacon grease

1 pound (450 g) white fish (such as tilapia, catfish, red snapper, or perch)

salt and pepper

1 pound (450 g) shrimp, crab, or bay scallops (can substitute more fish or sausage)

1 pound (450 g) andouille, boudin, chorizo, or smoked sausage

¾ cup (90 g) flour

1 large yellow onion, diced

3 cloves of garlic, minced

4 stalks of celery, diced

1 bell pepper, diced

¾ cup (90 g) okra, sliced

5 green onions, sliced

(1) 12-ounce (350-mL) can of diced tomatoes

2-½ quarts (2-⅓ L) hot chicken, fish, or vegetable stock

2 bay leaves

1 tablespoon (15 mL) Worcestershire sauce

2 tablespoons (14 g) fresh thyme, pulled from the stem

1 teaspoon (8 g) paprika

½ teaspoon (4 g) ground cayenne pepper

½ tsp (4 g) red pepper flakes

4 cups (946 g) cooked rice

Directions:

1. In a large soup pot, melt the butter or bacon grease. Add the celery, pepper, onions, and garlic. Cook over medium heat until the vegetables start to soften.
2. Add the flour a little at a time, stirring until incorporated. Cook until the flour starts to become golden in color.
3. Slowly add the stock, stirring constantly to prevent lumps from forming.
4. Add herbs and spices, sausage, canned tomatoes, okra, and Worcestershire sauce.
5. Let simmer for at least 30–45 minutes. Remember, the longer you let something simmer, the more the flavors will blend.
6. Add the fish and seafood, and bring up temperature to a low boil. Add green onions. Let cook until fish and seafood are cooked through (about 7 minutes). The fish should break apart easily with a spoon.
7. Serve in bowls over cooked rice, garnish with additional green onions or thyme.

* Adult supervision required.

Chapter 6

The Marvel of Mardi Gras

People celebrate this marvelous holiday in lots of ways! There are many traditions. Many schools have Mardi Gras parties. Students come in costumes and play games. Everyone enjoys eating king cakes.

King Cake and Other Ways to Celebrate

A king cake is a special Mardi Gras treat. It is a ring-shaped cake that has green, purple, and gold frosting.

King cakes also have a surprise inside them. A tiny plastic baby

Brazil's Carnival

One of the most famous Mardi Gras celebrations in the world occurs every year in Rio de Janeiro, Brazil. In Brazil, as well as in other countries around the world, this celebration is called Carnival.

25

doll is hidden in each cake. Someone's piece will have the toy in it. That person is supposed to bring the next king cake.

Some schools have Mardi Gras dances. They pick a Mardi Gras king and queen. Often schools have their own Mardi Gras parades, too. The students dress in costumes and parade on school grounds.

Libraries and museums also celebrate Mardi Gras. Stories may be read or crafts may be made. At the Louisiana Children's Museum in New Orleans, children make Mardi Gras masks.

Whoever gets the baby in the king cake will have good luck.

There are all kinds of Mardi Gras contests. Beauty and costume contests are common. Mardi Gras poster contests for young people are also popular.

Sporting events are enjoyed at this time, as well. Some cities have Mardi

Gras rugby tournaments. Rugby is a little like football. There are Mardi Gras marathons, too. A marathon is a long footrace. Each runner hopes to finish first. During Mardi Gras, the finish line may be painted in green, purple, and gold.

There are usually special events on the Monday before

Australia's Carnivals

Many people watch the wonderful and colorful Carnival parades each year in the Australian city of Sydney. There are floats and dancers, and everyone has a fun time!

Fat Tuesday. Lots of fun festivals are held. Some of the best parties, contests, and dances take place then. Often there are fireworks at night.

In some cities, there are parades that continue after dark. People fill the streets, and there is music everywhere. People wish the fun would never end. But at midnight after Fat Tuesday, the crowds go home and the cleanup begins.

One thing is certain. Mardi Gras will be just as great next year. This holiday is always filled with fun.

Mardi Gras Craft*

It does not matter where you live—anyone can catch the spirit of Mardi Gras! Making a Mardi Gras mask is a fun way to get in the spirit.

Here are the supplies you will need:

construction paper
popsicle sticks
glue
safety Scissors

glitter, sequins, feathers, or other decorations

Directions:

1. Draw a pattern on the construction paper big enough to cover your eyes. It can be in the shape of a cat, a bird, or anything you like.

2. Use the safety scissors to carefully cut along the lines you drew. Make sure that the holes for the eyes are big enough that you can see clearly out of them.

3. Turn your mask over to the back and use the glue to attach the popsicle stick to the mask. This will be your handle.

4. When the glue dries, turn the mask back over and use the sequins, glitter, and feathers to decorate it. Make it as colorful as possible. When the glue dries, you can use the mask for your own Mardi Gras fun!

Mardi Gras Mask

*Safety Note: Be sure to ask for help from an adult, if needed, to complete this project.

Glossary

boeuf gras—A fatted ox or bull. It stands for the last meat eaten before Lent begins.

captain—The leader of a Carnival club.

crest—An official design on an item such as a coin or helmet.

fast—To go an amount of time without eating.

king cake—A ring-shaped Mardi Gras cake with gold, purple, and green icing.

krewe—A Carnival club or group. Krewes often have Mardi Gras parades.

maskers—The costumed riders on Mardi Gras floats.

papier-mâché—A light, strong kind of paper mixed with glue that can be used to make things.

rugby—A type of football game that includes kicking, dribbling, and passing the ball in addition to tackling other players.

throws—Small objects that are thrown to the crowd during Mardi Gras parades.

Thousands of people can be in one parade. And thousands more come to watch!

Learn More

Books

Aloian, Molly. *Cultural Traditions in the United States.* New York: Crabtree Publishing, 2014.

McGee, Randel. *Paper Crafts for Mardi Gras* (Paper Craft Fun for Holidays). Berkeley Heights, NJ: Enslow Publishers, 2013. Kindle ed.

Murray, Julie. *Mardi Gras* (Buddy Books: Holidays). Minneapolis, MN: ABDO Publishing Company, 2014.

Peppas, Lynn. *Cultural Traditions in France.* St. Catharines, ON: Crabtree Publishing, 2014.

Websites

Holidays: Mardi Gras
ducksters.com/holidays/mardi_gras.php
  Check out facts and photos about Mardi Gras.

Mardi Gras on the Net
holidays.net/mardigras
  Learn more about Mardi Gras with recipes, crafts, facts, and more.

Mardi Gras
history.com/topics/holidays/mardi-gras
  Videos and photos help tell the story of Mardi Gras.

Index